S0-AFS-847

Sports Illustrated
JUDO

The Sports Illustrated Library

Sports Illustrated
JUDO

By PAUL STEWART

Photographs
by Heinz Kluetmeier

J. B. LIPPINCOTT COMPANY
New York

U.S. Library of Congress Cataloging in Publication Data

Stewart, Paul.
    Sports illustrated judo.

    (Sports illustrated library)
     1. Judo.   I. Kluetmeier, Heinz.   II. Sports illustrated
(Chicago)   III. Title.
GV475.S83   1976   796.8'152   75–15827
ISBN–0–397–01096–6
ISBN–0–397–01104–0 (pbk.)

Contents

Judo is the way to the most effective use of both mental and physical strength. By training you in attacks and defenses it refines your body and soul and helps you make the spiritual essence of judo a part of your very being. In this way, you are able to perfect yourself and contribute something of value to the world. This is the final goal of judo discipline.

—Jigoro Kano, founder of judo

Sports Illustrated

JUDO

1
The Fundamentals of the Sport

WHY JUDO? someone asked me. Why are you taking up judo at the age of thirty-five? My answer was simple. I wanted to revitalize my body, make it hard and supple. I wanted an outlet for my nervous energy. And above all, I wanted to train myself in self-defense.

All these years I had read about judo players who could throw men much larger than themselves. But was it true? Didn't the big man still hold all the advantages? No, he didn't, not in judo. With knowledge, training and sufficient strength, a small person can easily throw a larger opponent. A girl can throw a man, and an older man can defeat a much younger opponent, for judo is the strategic use of one's strength.

Let's take a very graphic illustration. One day at my class, a powerful young giant was enrolled: 6 feet 4 inches in his bare feet and weighing somewhere in the vicinity of 220 pounds. I weigh 170 pounds, and, while I am in good shape, I was in nowhere near this man's physical condition.

He's too much for me to handle, I thought. Just then my instructor told me to play with this man. We bowed, and my opponent rushed me, much like the semiprofessional football player he was. Instinctively I gave way—the classic judo answer to an aggressive rush—falling backward to the mat. At the same time I had grabbed his lapels and placed my foot in his stomach, pulling him even more at me. He went flying over my head, doing a magnificent somersault in midair, and landed on his back with a thunderous crash. I had used *tomoe nage* on him.

When you are studying judo with other people and practicing with them, your moves have to be better, sharper and more precise than you would ordinarily need for self-defense. After all, the judo player knows you are going to try to throw. But in self-defense, no one is going to expect the kind of moves you can borrow from judo; you are going to have the element of surprise. As self-defense, judo can be devastating.

But, as good a weapon as judo is, the student—whether man, woman or child—will discover a strange contradiction as he studies the sport. He will gain tremendous confidence, peace of mind and the feeling that one has nothing to prove with a fight. Many instructors have never used judo in self-defense. My teacher told me, "I have been able to walk away from any fight. I don't have to prove myself."

Of all the instructors I have come in contact with, none has ever impressed me as much as a quiet teacher now living in New Jersey.

Yoshisada Yonezuka is deceptive. He's not especially large, broad-shouldered or intense. To the contrary, Yone is calm, almost to the point of being sleepy-eyed.

As I stood across the mat from Yone, at his Judo and Karate Center in Cranford, New Jersey, I felt almost cocky. He's almost the same height, the same weight as I am, and he's in early middle age. I've got a chance, I thought. We were ready to participate in *randori*, or fighting practice.

We saluted each other with a bow. Now this sixth-degree

black-belt master of judo and black-belt expert in karate and I, a first-degree brown-belt in judo, moved in.

It was an illuminating experience. Here was an advanced master in judo who did not bear in with his strength, who kept what appeared to be a loose grip. His attention was not all on me. He attempted one throw while pointing out something to another student. He missed, so I tried a move. I got nowhere. Still talking to that student, he tried again. Somehow I felt the tremendous power, the speed of the throw, but I desperately clung to his legs, and he tripped a little over me.

It must have shocked him. He grunted and shook my lapels. Suddenly I was flying through the air, a victim of the perfect *ippon seoi nage*. The throw had been executed with speed and flawless technique—a perfect exhibition of the fundamentals of judo. Again and again I went down until I signaled I was through.

I look upon that day as my first lesson in judo, the gentle sport. Yone is a man of phenomenal strength, but that

Throughout the pages of this book, you'll see Yone carefully demonstrate the most important fundamentals of judo, assisted by one of his students, Clyde Worthen, himself a fourth-degree black-belt champion.

13

strength is turned on only at the precise second it's needed. He is also a man of pantherlike quickness, so fast that, while you can see him moving in for a throw, you cannot summon up your reflexes to counter his attack. And above all, he exploits your weakness. If you are standing too far forward— or if you're too far back, too aggressive or too timid—Yone uses a technique that capitalizes on that error.

As a young man, Yone was an All-Northern Japan champion. Now he has twice won the annual U.S. masters tournament. He also defeated seven black-belt judo experts, one by one, when he was blind-folded during an exhibition. An impressive master of judo, he's equally impressive as a teacher. His moves are the essence of simplicity, speed and, of course, power. But if anything, Yone is a man of fundamentals.

THE JAPANESE HERITAGE OF JUDO

Judo is a remnant of ancient Japan. This was the land of the samurai, those swaggering, sword-carrying knights who roamed through the ancient Japanese countryside. This was also a land of courtesy, respect for one's elders, and an intense feeling for the ceremonious act itself.

Centuries ago, Japan was a feudal society. There were warlords, each with his own army. There were also schools for learning how to battle with swords, bows and arrows, clubs, spears, and with one's bare hands. Jujitsu is the art of fighting with one's hands, and in ancient Japan it had been developed into a lethal science. But slowly the ancient martial arts began to disappear. Japan entered modern times. Newer and more efficient weapons were established. Commodore Perry's visit to Japan in the mid-1850's changed Japanese civilization.

However, in 1882 a man named Jigoro Kano decided to rethink the techniques of jujitsu. He removed its dangerous elements, such as the foot and hand strikes. Kano called his new sport judo, which means "the gentle way." To the uninitiated

14

this would seem an obvious contradiction. How can such a sport be considered gentle?

Here is what Kano said:

> . . . let us suppose that we estimate the strength of man in units of one. Let us say that the strength of a man standing in front of me is represented by ten units whereas my strength, less than his, is represented by seven units. Now, if he pushes me with all his force I shall certainly be pushed back or thrown down, even if I use all my strength against his. . . . But if, instead of opposing him, I were to give way to his strength by withdrawing my body just as much as he had pushed, taking care at the same time to keep my balance, then he would naturally lean forward and thus lose his balance.
>
> In this new position, he may have become so weak (not in actual physical strength but because of his awkward position) as to have his strength represented for the moment by only three units, instead of his normal ten units. But meanwhile, by keeping my balance, I retain my full strength, as originally represented by seven units. Here then I am momentarily in a superior position, and can defeat my opponent by using only half my strength, that is half of my seven units, or three and one-half, against his three. This leaves one-half of my strength available for any purpose. Now, if I had greater strength than my opponent I could of course push him back. But even if I wished to push him back and had the power to do so, it would still be better for me first to give way, because by so doing I should have greatly economised my energy and exhausted my opponent's.

That passage reveals the true secret of all techniques of judo: maneuvering a stronger opponent into a position where he cannot use his full strength against you and where you may use your full strength to greatest advantage.

So in judo you must learn to capitalize on your opponent's weaknesses. If he's too tall, he may find it difficult to execute certain throws. If he is too heavy, he's apt to be slower than you. You'll learn to capitalize even on an opponent's emotions. If a player rushes at you too aggressively, you will learn the moves which will both blunt his attack and cause

15

his own downfall. Judo requires great finesse, coordination of the entire body, concentration of thought, and, finally, concentration of power. Often a tiny thing means success or failure for a judo player. Your arms must push or pull, your legs clip, sweep, hook or chop. Your head must guide the entire set of maneuvers. Quickly. Decisively. And with precision. Only when all these factors are involved will a judo player succeed.

WHAT TO EXPECT

If you decide to study judo, here's what happens:

First, you must learn the terminology of the sport. It's harder than most. It's all in Japanese, naturally. For instance, you will learn in a *dojo*. That's the studio or gym. The *sensei* is your instructor. You'll be wearing a *gi*, a coat and pants made of rugged, heavy cotton.

The next thing you'll learn is courtesy. The very fact that a bow, or *rei*, is important says something about the sport of

In a standing bow, a judo player places his arms at his sides and bows from the waist, slowly and with gentleness.

16

In a kneeling bow, the judo player starts by kneeling and then crossing his feet. Next, he places his palms on his thighs, with his knees slightly spread. Now he bends downward, placing his palms on the mat in front of his knees; his elbows are out and forward of his body.

judo. This bow indicates the physical courtesy and respect one has toward another student, his opponent or his *sensei*. You bow when you enter the *dojo*, mostly as a measure of respect for this learning place. The class starts with a bow. In *randori*, you must bow before and after each match. The class ends with a bow. This respect is an important lesson. Respect toward other people in judo, respect toward your opponent and, ultimately, respect for oneself. But most important, this disciplined courtesy helps instill control of one's emotions. In one instance, you may fight aggressively and vigorously; in the next, exhibit the helpfulness one should toward another student interested in learning a throw.

After the *rei*, you'll immediately go into warming-up exercises, first stretching the back, hands, legs, and neck. Loosening and stretching these muscles is important, as it helps prevent injuries. You'll encounter enormous stresses and strains in judo, and your muscles, if properly warmed up, will be that much more resilient.

17

Stretching exercise for your back.

Stretching your neck muscles.

Stretching your legs.

HOW TO FALL

Ukemi, or falling practice, is the first and one of the most important areas of study—for good reason, since you'll be falling a lot. Falling is part of judo. You'll be thrown as often as you throw somebody else, and learning how to fall can prevent injuries, especially when you gain the confidence in knowing how that comes only with practice.

It pays to practice falling at every lesson. Learn the essential techniques and practice them over and over again until they are automatic reflexes. The first essential is: always tuck your chin in. This helps to prevent any shock to the back of your head when you land on your back. The second essential: always try to spread the shock of impact over as large an area of your body as possible. Land on your back if you can, and develop the habit of always slapping the mat. Doing these things can be tough at first, but if you practice falling again and again, the proper fall will become instinctive and easy.

Sometimes you will find it is far better to let yourself be thrown when your cause is lost than to keep fighting. If you don't fall so as to land safely on your back, you may land on your knees, which are more vulnerable to injury.

To fall from a sitting position, raise your arms (opposite page) and start to fall back (top). Just as your back is about to hit, slap the mat hard with both forearms. This helps break your fall. Remember to keep your chin tucked in. Practice this fall from a standing position and a squatting position.

21

Left to right: to fall sideways, lie on your back, raise your legs and roll to one side. Slap the mat on the side you are turning to. Keep your chin tucked in on this fall too, to protect your head and neck. Now do the same thing on the other side. Practice this fall as much as possible because you will be thrown this way hundreds of times.

Left to-right: to tumble forward in the judo roll, place your hands on the side of your lead foot. Tuck the lead shoulder in to prevent it from hitting the mat. Push with your feet and tumble. Again, keep your chin tucked in. As you start to land on your back, slap the mat with your arm as hard as you can.

HOW TO STAND

Above all, you must have a stance in which you are comfortable. Your body should be relaxed but not limp. You must be able to move quickly and strongly from your stance. For an offensive stance, your feet should be slightly apart, hands at your sides. Your posture, in total effect, is erect. You can lead slightly with your right or left foot if it is more comfortable or more advantageous to you. It is less tiring to stand in this natural posture, and it is a remarkably effective position from which to apply throws.

In defending against an opponent's throw, spread your feet wider, bend your knees and lower your body. From this lower posture, it is easier to resist a technique. To counter a sweeping hip throw, sink lower and turn your hip against your opponent. However, you should also remember that you do not win a match on defensive play alone; this

Shizen tai. At left is shown the ideal position for offensive judo. The players are relaxed but ready to spring into action. At right: the perfect defensive position in judo. By bending your knees and placing your feet further apart, you are lowering your center of gravity. It will be hard for anyone to penetrate your defense easily. This stance has an obvious shortcoming: it's an ineffectual way to start an attack of your own.

deep, defensive stance puts you into an awkward offensive posture. It is hard to execute throws from this position.

HOW TO MOVE

It is unwise to walk naturally across the mat. Move your body across it with short, sliding steps. Never cross your feet as you move. It would be relatively easy for an opponent to apply a foot sweep against you. Your balance must be low. To that end, keeping your feet on the mat as long as you can will certainly help you defend against throws.

YOUR GRIP

Many techniques involve the use of the *gi*. As you grip your opponent's *gi*, you should grip strongly, but not so strongly as to tire your arms and hands. For a moment, pretend you are gripping a screwdriver. You will notice you grip with the three smaller fingers; your thumb and index finger are used as guides. That's precisely the way you grip the lapel of your opponent's *gi*. Thumb and index finger should remain loose, the other three tight.

In a normal grip, you will grip his left lapel with your

right hand, keeping your upper arm close to your body. Your left hand grips his right sleeve, somewhere around the elbow. Your grip must be comfortable to you; it, like the stance, depends upon the individual. If you play a smaller person, you may find it more comfortable to grip the back of his *gi*. For your own protection, you may not grip the end of your opponent's sleeve or pants. It would be easy for him to twist and perhaps injure your hand.

RANDORI

The last part of a lesson is *randori,* or fighting practice. Now you will be expected to apply your knowledge of judo against an opponent. The most common mistake is to try to battle too hard. The *randori* is practice; the *shiai* is the contest. If you are going to improve your judo, you must not be afraid of trying new and more difficult techniques even if you will be effectively countered or even thrown to the mat. Simply accept the fact that you will be thrown—many times. Practice your throws; vary your attack. First one throw, then another. A feint. Try to take advantage of a flaw in your opponent's defense. Many players, perhaps afraid of losing face in practice, simply go into an extreme defensive crouch. True, it may be hard to throw them, but it is equally hard for them to throw an opponent. Your progress in judo will depend on how well and how thoroughly you use *randori.* Practice with as many different players, big and small, as you can in the course of a *randori.* You'll find that each judo player has a different style, and it becomes a challenge to outwit him strategically.

UCHIKOMI

Uchikomi is form practice. It follows the calisthenics and warming up. You will be expected to practice your throws, hold-downs or chokes. The instructor usually moves from person to person, advising each one how to throw better. Generally the *sensei* matches you with someone of equivalent size. As a rule, your opponent lets you in, enabling you to practice the throws. And you, as a rule, do not follow through with your throws. You'll exchange throws with your partner, working on timing, footwork, grips—always working to make the throws instinctive.

NE WAZA

Many people think judo consists of throwing only, but this is far from the truth. *Ne Waza,* or fighting on the mat, is a large part of the sport and includes an enormous variety of hold-downs, armlocks and choking techniques. In mat work judo is similar to wrestling. Typically mat-work exercises might consist of practices where partners sit back to back and, at the count of three, whirl and try to immobilize the opponent with an armlock or choke him into submission. Or you might be allowed to put a hold-down on an opponent which he will try to break. Mat work builds stamina and strength. Also, since some players feel more comfortable on the mat and will go there instead of trying to throw you, you should work as much at this aspect of the sport as at throwing.

SHIAI

The ultimate test of your skill is, of course, against an opponent in an actual contest. In judo, such a contest is called a *shiai.* Depending on your belt rank, matches are 3 to 6 minutes in length. You play on a 20-by-20-foot mat under the supervision of a referee and two judges. The object of a match is to score one point, an *ippon*, on your opponent. You can score an *ippon* with one clean throw or

27

if the throw isn't a good one, you might score a *waza ari,* a half-point.

You can also win by a hold-down, a choke or an armlock. In a hold-down, you win by controlling your opponent for 30 seconds. In a choke or an armlock, your opponent must give up. He taps the mat with a hand or foot, or says "*Mat-tai,*" meaning "enough."

Children may enter judo contests when they are five years old. In the photograph above, you see two six-year-old boys practicing for their first *shiai.*

You can also win a match simply on an accumulation of *waza aris.* Two such half-points would win the match. Or, if your opponent is too defensive-minded, you could win merely on aggressiveness.

There are a variety of *shiais* in the United States. You will be matched with other people according to your size and your belt rank. Competing in a *shiai* is tremendously excit-ing; it's also useful in perfecting your techniques.

Ippon! It looks like a powerful throw, one that almost certainly will win the match.

You can win a match by mat work too. If you are on the mat you can win with an armlock, a choke or holding down (controlling) your opponent.

2
Throwing
Techniques:

NAGE WAZA

A WELL-EXECUTED JUDO THROW is put together with timing and precision. Ideally, you'll step in, whirl and pull your opponent player onto your hips, sweeping him off his feet and down on the mat with your legs. Deceptively simple. But before you can actually throw a player, you need to know how to stand, how to move on the mat, how to grip your opponent's *gi*, how to break his balance and, finally, how to actually get him off his feet and onto the mat. Strategically, you can take advantage of a sudden lunge by your opponent. As he lunges, he'll be vulnerable to an attack, since he'll be off balance and unable to retaliate with his full strength. You'll discover the kinds of throws to use in such a situation.

Or you can start the action. Push your opponent hard. He may push back just as hard. If he does, he may be opening himself up. You'll learn how the push-pull principle operates. If you pull someone onto your back, you'll be pushing against his legs. The object is to put your opponent on a horizontal plane. If you pull his torso to one side, you'll sweep his legs to the other. In many throws, the laws of mechanics operate so clearly that you may understand the art of throwing better if you think of it in these terms. In a number of throws, the primary object is to get under your opponent, pulling him off his feet and onto your hip. Then you'll throw him off that hip or off your back. Think of your hip or back as a lever. If you get under him far enough, you won't need much force to throw him to the mat. But if you don't get deep enough, you may not be able to throw him at all.

Breaking Your Opponent's Balance: Kuzushi

This is the key to a throw in judo. Success comes to the player who understands how to finesse his opponent into breaking his natural balance. If his weight is on his heels, he cannot attack you. He is also susceptible to an attack from you. If his weight is on his toes, he has lost his offense, however temporarily. Again he is vulnerable.

You can break your opponent's balance in a number of directions if you push or pull him. You can push him quickly and, if he resists, pull him forward on his toes and execute a throw. Or pull him first and, as he resists your pull by putting his weight on his heels, push him.

Your opponent can literally break his own balance. One player I knew would start huffing and puffing before he got ready to execute his throw. I could sense the throw coming, and as it came, I would backpedal to counter. If he failed to throw me, his weight was directly on his toes. Then I had him.

Always throw a player in the direction in which he is moving. If a player always leans forward, throw him forward; you simply will not be able to throw him backward.

Timing the Moment of Your Throw

Your opponent is most vulnerable to an attack when he is stepping forward or backward, pivoting to his right or left the split second before he tries to throw you, or when you counter his throw.

As you counter his *harai goshi*, for example, you can move in slightly behind him and trip him backward. Or you can step in front of him for a *harai goshi* of your own.

OSOTO GARI

Of all judo throws, *osoto gari* is the easiest to learn and execute. Properly done, it is a devastatingly powerful throw. But even when it isn't executed correctly, a judo player can make *osoto gari* work for him.

Its strategy is startlingly simple: try to push your opponent's weight onto one foot, and then sweep that leg out from under him, pushing him backward at the same time. As you'll see on the following pages, *osoto gari* illustrates three basic concepts of judo—opportunity, anticipation, co-ordination—which in turn demonstrate why judo is the gentle way.

Opportunity

If you are using *osoto gari* to throw an opponent, you must be sure you can reach the target: his leg. Consequently, if your opponent consistently leads with his right foot, he may be vulnerable to *osoto gari*. As you play other students in *randori* and *shiai*, you'll spot many opportunities. Take advantage of them.

But as you compete in higher ranks, you will have to create your own opportunity. In *osoto gari*, if you pull your opponent to the left, he'll resist, possibly even putting more weight on that right foot. Then strike.

Anticipation

Once you've taken advantage of or created your own opportunity, timing becomes essential. Timing a strike should be second nature. You should try to throw your opponent the instant before he starts a throw or starts to defend himself against a feint of yours. In this way, judo becomes much like a chess game, in which you try to think out your opponent's strategy and then take advantage of it. For example, imagine that your right foot is vulnerable for an *osoto gari*. Suddenly you realize that your opponent has spotted this opening, and you know, instinctively, he is

33

coming at you with *osoto gari*. If it looks to be a weak effort, you could counter with a more powerful *osoto gari* of your own. Or, if he's powerful at this technique, you should attempt a throw of your own.

Coordination

Each judo throw is as carefully choreographed as a dance step. All parts of the body must act in unison. If your leg sweeps an opponent's leg out from under him, as in *osoto gari*, then your arms push his torso backward. The ultimate aim is to put your opponent on a horizontal plane so that he may fall as quickly as possible. As you sweep his feet to one side or another, pull his *osoto gari* the other way.

Left: "Get your grip," judo players often call out in competition. Yone's left hand grips the outside of his opponent's right arm. His right hand is on his opponent's lapel. He is alert for an opportunity to execute *osoto gari.*

Center: Yone spots an opening and steps deep to the outside of his opponent's right foot with his left foot. Simultaneously, Yone's right arm brings his opponent's torso forward.

Opposite, right: Yone's right leg follows his left to the outside, swinging past his opponent's right leg into a high arc.

Left: as he brings his right leg down and into his opponent's leg, his right arm suddenly reverses the pressure. Instead of pulling his opponent into him, he pushes back and up against his opponent's neck.

Center: as Yone brings his right leg down, he points his foot. This serves to increase the downward momentum of his leg. As his thigh hits the back of his opponent's thigh, Yone's forehead falls straight at the mat. All of his tremendous strength is channeled into the leg sweep and the arm push, all of which will send his opponent onto that horizontal plane and crashing to the mat.

Right: because the opponent is swept so cleanly off his one foot, he simply cannot resist. But in many cases your opponent will be able to block your first effort. If so, relax your pressure for a fraction of a second; your opponent may be fooled into thinking you've given up. Then try another *osoto gari*. It usually works if you put enough power into it.

At right: Yone places his foot in between his opponent's legs, moving it in a circular motion to hook the back of his opponent's knee. Yone points his toes so that the back of his heel forms a hook and locks his foot successfully in an *ouchi gari*.

Above: Yone spots an opportunity for *ouchi gari*. His opponent is not in a secure defensive stance. He is standing in too erect a posture, susceptible to a leg throw. To create an even better opening, Yone pulls his opponent's right sleeve forward and pushes his left lapel. He has made his opponent wonder what Yone is going to do. The opponent decides to resist and brings his left foot forward, right into Yone's trap.

Yone's right hand, with a firm grip, holds his opponent's left lapel and pushes him back and to the left. Yone's left hand pushes his opponent in that same direction.

OUCHI GARI

Ouchi gari, like *osoto gari*, is a good leg throw to master quickly, as it is a simple and effective move. The aim of this movement is to hook the inside of your opponent's leg and pull that leg toward you. As you do this, you'll push his torso back, attempting to put your opponent on that horizontal plane.

Typically, a player will get the hook on his opponent's leg and simply not hook hard enough. Or, in trying to hook his opponent's leg, a player will forget to push against the opponent's torso.

Perhaps a player will get the hook, exert the powerful push and yet completely abandon the move when his opponent puts up resistance. An experienced player will not give up. He'll continue to hook and push to try to keep driving his opponent back across the mat. Essentially, you'll be hopping on one foot; he'll be forced into hopping backward on one foot (your foot will keep his other foot entrapped in that hooking motion). As long as you maintain that driving pressure, you'll maintain your equilibrium. But he may very well fall.

The maneuver is completed as Yone follows with the torso push and the leg hook. There is no way the falling player can resist this effective throw now.

HIZA GARUMA

Hiza garuma is a sudden move that depends almost completely on speed for its effectiveness. It's valuable to learn this move as soon as possible and continue to practice it at every session. *Hiza garuma* startles opponents and can "loosen" an opponent up for a strong second throw such as *harai goshi* or *uchi mata*.

At left is shown the critical point of *hiza garuma*. You should slap the sole of your striking foot against your opponent's kneecap. You'll see how Yone almost cradles his opponent's kneecap with the sole of his foot. He is managing to deliver the maximum slap against that vulnerable spot.

At right, Yone steps in and to the side with his left foot, pivoting when necessary to provide a base from which to strike out with his right foot.

Below left: as he pivots, Yone's right foot sweeps out in a straight line. The sole of his right foot slaps against his opponent's left kneecap. You will see how Yone uses his arms to strengthen the force of his *hiza garuma.* In a lifting, pulling movement, he seeks to shift his opponent's weight onto that leg under attack.

Below right: he has forced his opponent onto the one foot. In effect, his opponent's body is going to revolve around his left kneecap. Yone uses his arms as if he were turning the steering wheel of a car.

Armed with a good grip, Yone steps forward with his right foot.

With his right foot in pivoting position (below), Yone pulls hard on his opponent's right sleeve to throw him off balance. With his right hand, he is going deep behind his opponent's neck.

KOSHI GARUMA

Faced with a taller opponent, Yone attacks with *koshi garuma*, a fast, powerful hip throw. And, like all hip throws, it requires the same footwork to get "inside." Practice those steps as often as you can. First, step inside and slightly ahead of your opponent's right foot, pivot with that foot and bring your left foot back inside your opponent's legs.

Now, once you're inside, you can grab him around the waist (*ogoshi*), sweep his leg out from under him (*harai goshi*) or grab your opponent around his neck and throw him off your hip (*koshi garuma*).

Watch how fast and how powerfully Yone attacks his opponent with *koshi garuma* in the sequence of photographs on these pages.

Here Yone has his opponent "floating" on his hip, ready to throw him down on the mat.

Ippon!

:h a good inside position (left), ne now has it all together: low hip ition to give him plenty of lifting wer; a tough grip around his oppo- 1t's neck for pulling him onto his . Yone's left arm helps to unbalance opponent, pulling him ahead and ward.

OKURI ASHI BARAI

This foot sweep does not involve tremendous power; it requires good timing and good speed. You sweep your opponent's feet in the direction he is moving and pull his torso in the opposite direction. Once again, this push-pull force will put your opponent on a horizontal plane.

It is a simple maneuver and can be used as an offensive move in itself or as a good follow-through when another throw is blocked. In *okuri ashi barai* you can sweep from either side, using your right or left foot. Always slap your opponent's feet away from his body, striking with the sole of your foot.

Yone is creating his opportunity, moving his opponent from side to side, from front to back. If his opponent is wary of leaning too much in one direction, Yone has a chance of helping him go in that direction with an immediate *okuri ashi barai*. Or, if Yone pushes his opponent hard into one direction, he can strike the split second before his opponent counters with a push back.

Yone strikes with the sole of his foot against a point just below his opponent's ankle bone. (Concentrate on keeping your foot low by trying to make a slight noise on the mat with that foot.) Here Yone has just delivered the foot slap; the opponent's foot is forced up off the mat.

Here you see just how effective Yone's arms are. He uses his left hand to lift his opponent up and away from his feet; his right hand pulls him down and away from his feet. This striking foot continues to follow through, sweeping his opponent's feet clearly out from under him.

Yone has combined arm push-pull with a quick, hard foot slap to put his opponent onto that horizontal plane. *Okuri ashi barai,* with its reliance on timing rather than strength, represents the quintessence of "the gentle sport."

In judo, force should be directed precisely. If a throw calls for the use of both arms, you cannot expect to throw an opponent using only one arm. See at right the tension in the cloth of the *gi;* it will give you an idea how much pull Yone exerts with his right arm. The other arm lifts the opponent up and off his feet.

KOSOTO GARI

By learning a relatively simple foot sweep such as *kosoto gari*, you can gain a deep and valuable insight into judo. To be able to react quickly, either defensively or offensively, a player must be relaxed and alert. If you're too tense, you can't feel what your opponent may do next.

Almost all beginners, many intermediates and a surprising

Above: Yone has created a perfect opening for *kosoto gari* simply by maneuvering his opponent on the mat. As his opponent steps forward with his left foot, Yone steps to the side with his right foot. Now, at the very instant his opponent lifts his right foot to take a step forward, Yone is ready to strike with his left foot. Yone's left foot is slightly angled to the right, enabling him to get a good position for the strike.

First (below), Yone delivers the fo slap with his left foot, striking h opponent's heel with the sole of th foot. The slap should be low a hard. You should either try to ma a slightly audible noise on the m (as Yone is doing here) or execute short, powerful sweep upward. T choice is yours, and it depends up a fine point: if your opponent's fo is off the mat, sweep upward; if is firmly planted, sweep it along t mat.

number of top judo players simply try to overpower their opponents. Such a strategy may work in a local *dojo*, but in a major *shiai*, never!

Yone is enormously powerful, and yet he plays lightly until he sees his opening. He conserves his energy by not playing as hard as he could for every second of the match. In so doing, he has also startled his opponent with such sudden power.

While Yone has successfully followed through with his foot sweep, he has also used his arms very effectively to pull his opponent's torso backward. His left arm exerts strong pressure on his opponent's right sleeve. His right arm pulls his opponent's lapel backward into a very awkward position.

Yone is putting his opponent into a horizontal position. With his legs out from under him, his torso pushed backward, the player falls to the mat.

KOUCHI GARI

If your timing isn't flawless, you'll seldom get *kouchi gari* on your opponent. While the elements of the move itself are simple, the mastery of the timing takes time and practice. The photographs of this move show how Yone catches his opponent off guard, and then, with incredible speed and force, hurls his entire body into the move. Again,

Like any advanced player, Yone moves decisively. Here, he has spotted a weakness in his opponent's defense. His opponent has just put his foot down a little too far forward. His weight appears to be on the heel of that extremely vulnerable right foot. (You can also catch an unwary player when he's stepping backward.)

With pantherlike speed, Yone pounces upon his opponent's temporary lapse. He spins on his left foot and whips his right foot around, slapping it against his opponent's right heel. The more weight your opponent has on that heel, the more effective your strike will be. Simultaneously, Yone is using his arms to upset his opponent's balance. His right arm pushes back and then down. His left arm pulls his opponent down toward the mat.

kouchi gari involves the basic principle of forcing an opponent's weight onto one leg, and then sweeping that leg out from under the opponent.

There are two excellent reasons for practicing and mastering *kouchi gari*. One is obvious: it's a good move. The other is subtle: *kouchi gari* is a quick move to fake an opponent with first and then follow up with a powerful hip throw.

Many times, a good judo player starts a move and, then, because of what looks like determined resistance, gives up halfway through the move.

To succeed, you must follow through. With your right foot, you must bring your opponent's foot toward you. Similarly, you must follow through with your arms. Like Yone, you must commit yourself to the throw, striving with every motion to bring your opponent down.

47

IPPON SEOI NAGE

For *ippon seoi nage* to be effective, a judo player has to execute the throw with speed and power—particularly speed. You have to be able to get "inside" without telegraphing the move to your opponent, since *ippon seoi nage* can be easily blocked. But once "inside," an experienced black-belt such as Yone will get his throw easily.

Look for the opportunity; your opponent may have a "stiff" arm, or may simply be leaning too far forward. To create the opportunity, try to bait an opponent by a push. A fraction of a second before he returns the push, step in for the *ippon seoi nage.* At the same time, grab his sleeve with one hand and put the other under that same arm, as high up on his arm as you can get.

As you step—or in some cases hop in, you must pivot on your lead foot and bring the other foot back between your opponent's legs. As you practice this entry, make the step, pivot, and bend your knees.

Above, left: sometimes in judo you have to slam your opponent with your hips. In *ippon seoi nage* the trick is to come in low and then, once in position, straighten your legs and hips, making your opponent bounce up out of his position and eventually onto your back.

Above, right: as soon as you pivot into position, slip your arm under his armpit and lock it with the crook of your elbow. The higher up you can get your arm, the tighter a grip you will have on your opponent. It is this arm lever, of course, which helps you get your opponent up on your back. If you feel as though the throw is coming off your heels, you will not be getting the kind of power you need to throw somebody successfully. You must throw off your toes.

Below: once you have your opponent off his feet, it is a simple matter to drop him to the floor. With one hand you are pulling him onto your back; with the other you are pulling down and off. Under such pressure he will slam onto his back on the mat.

SEOI NAGE

Seoi nage is a powerful weapon against a taller, heavier opponent, as it provides the smaller man with enormous leverage.

In *seoi nage* you are going to get your opponent on your back and then use both hands to throw him off and onto the mat. For the throw to be effective, the attacker must be low. For one thing, it is far easier to get a person onto your back from a low position. For another, if you are shorter than your opponent, you have that much more of an advantage over him.

While the footwork and the use of the hips are strikingly similar to that of *ippon seoi nage*, you will be using your hands and arms in a completely different manner. As you pull his left sleeve with your right hand, your right hand *twists* into your opponent's lapel. That twisting motion allows you to pull really hard. Now, with your right hand twisting, pull that arm forward. Your right elbow very naturally falls into his left armpit, and that provides you with a lot of leverage for the throw.

At right, Yone has a good right-hand grip on his opponent's lapel, which must be loose. (Shake it several times a moment or two before you attempt *seoi nage* so you are sure to have enough play in it to twist with your right hand.) Yone's left hand has a good grip on his opponent's right sleeve.

Yone has stepped in with his
right foot, the same way he would
enter for an *ippon seoi nage*.
Similarly, his left arm pulls his
opponent's right arm out and up,
unweighting his opponent. At this
instant his right hand is twisting
into his opponent's lapel.

As Yone gets inside and low, he
pivots, spinning on his right foot,
and brings his left foot deep inside his opponent's legs. His hips
are almost level with his opponent's knees.

The "low" position is the key to successful *seoi nage:* it allows a good hip lift and it also makes it easier to pull your opponent onto your back. Once he is on your back, he is completely vulnerable to the throw.

To throw his opponent, Yone has done nothing more than straighten his legs and pull with both arms. With plenty of leverage in his arms and hips, he can easily get him onto his back.

Once you're into a throw, finish it out. In *seoi nage,* you simply pull as hard as you can, using both arms. If your opponent resists, you may be able to throw by dropping to one or both of your knees, which may force him to fall over you. Be sure to pull your opponent over your shoulder and straight down. If you throw him to the side, you'll weaken your throw.

OGOSHI

As a very accomplished sixth-degree black-belt, Yone can usually get any throw he wants at any time on anyone less than world-caliber champions. He undoubtedly can use *ogoshi* very effectively whenever he wants to. However, many players find it difficult to use on anyone but beginners—someone who is really open, completely disregarding his defensive posture.

As in any hip throw, you lead with your right foot, placing it slightly ahead of your opponent's right foot. You pivot on that foot and bring your left foot deep inside your opponent's legs. In the photograph at left Yone shows clearly how he reaches around his opponent's waist the second he steps in with that right foot. Simultaneously, he uses his left hand to bring his opponent's right arm up and out. This has the effect of unweighting his opponent, making him easier to pick up and throw.

What is unweighting all about? At right, below, Yone has pulled his opponent up with his left hand, pushing him up with his hips, all with the purpose of unweighting him from the mat. Once his opponent is unweighted, Yone has a firm right arm around his waist and can roll him off his hips with ease. To get more lifting power with your legs, try to straighten them with a spring or snap.

But *ogoshi* can be a unique weapon for you as a second throw. Suppose you tried an *osoto gari*. Your opponent would immediately pull back, and at that point he might be off balance. Or, suppose he tries a move on you and fails. At that point, he would most likely be off balance and susceptible to an *ogoshi*.

The opponent is thrown off Yone's right shoulder, over his hips and down in front of him.

Now with his opponent actually off his feet, Yone prepares to throw him off his hips.

His opponent hits the mat; Yone remains on his feet, ready to slide into a hold-down, choke or armlock.

At left, Yone, who can go to either side for an attack, decides to strike against his opponent's left side.

Having stepped forward with his striking foot (above right), Yone pivots on it. This photo shows the interplay of a co-ordinated arm-and-leg attack. Yone's left arm is pulling his opponent forward.

HARAI GOSHI

When you watch a black-belt throw an opponent with this amazingly powerful hip throw, the maneuver looks deceptively simple. It isn't. *Harai goshi* requires a combination of speed, muscle, balance and superb coordination. *Harai goshi* looks unstoppable. It is. Once an acknowledged master like Yone gets "in" on a player, he is going to throw him.

Developing a Successful Harai Goshi

The key to this throw lies in steady practice of its opening steps. First, step slightly forward with your left foot and pivot on that foot. Now step back deeply with your right foot, pretending to place it in between your opponent's feet. The key is to step deeply enough, for you will be balancing on that right foot, and, for adequate power and balance, you should be on the ball of that foot. If you don't step deeply enough, you will not have a powerful platform

56

The footwork is critical in *harai goshi*. At left, Yone's left foot has completed the pivot and his right one is going deep between his opponent's legs.

Now Yone's other leg sweeps back against the opponent's left leg. The combination arm pull and leg sweep takes the opponent off his feet and onto Yone's hip. As the opponent rolls off Yone's hip (at center), you can clearly see why that right foot (in a left-side attack) must be placed securely and properly. For an instant, both men are balanced on Yone's right leg.

Right: using his arms, Yone completes the throw by driving his opponent down onto the mat.

for the throw and will feel as though you are being pulled backward.

Once you have mastered the rhythm of the steps, practice the feeling of pulling your opponent toward you with your left arm. With your right arm, pull his left arm forward.

Yone explains the importance of a good grip to his student: "Grab a lot of material. It will give you a stronger grip." He has reached around his student's neck to grab deep onto his shoulder. The other hand will grip tightly onto the student's arm for the powerful pull, which unbalances the student forward. Notice also how closely Yone fits in against the student—as close as possible to provide the turning point.

UTSURI GOSHI

There are extraordinary opportunities in judo for the player who prepares himself against his opponent's attack. Surprise can count as much as strength. By executing an unexpected maneuver, a beginning player can defeat a black-belt.

For example, you know that at some point your opponent will attempt an *uchi mata,* an *osoto gari* or a *harai goshi* against you. Surprise him with a countermove. For example, when a player attacks you with a *harai goshi,* you can block his attack successfully with a simple move: throwing your hips into his hips and jutting them out ahead of your body. With timing, strength and a technique called *utsuri goshi,* you can throw him.

In the following sequence of photographs, you can clearly see how Yone has stopped his student's *harai goshi* and countered successfully with *utsuri goshi.*

Good players that they are, Yone and his student work at getting good, hard grips in a *randori.*

The student quickly attempts to use *harai goshi* on Yone. He steps in against his *sensei* and tries to grab him around his neck.

Because he is in such a low position, Yone can lift the student easily with his legs. In this position on Yone's hips, the student is obviously vulnerable to *utsuri goshi*.

To block this throw, Yone quickly sinks into a deep, defensive crouch and, just as the student attempts to get back into position, wraps his arms tightly around the student's waist.

As he holds the student high on his hips, Yone brings his left hip around to the right, switching the relative position of his opponent in midair.

As Yone moves his left hip around, he twists and drops the student onto that hip, still holding him tightly around the waist. He has put the student on a horizontal plane.

With his arms, Yone throws his opponent to the right, off that left hip. Yone completes *utsuri goshi* by throwing the student on his back for a clean point, an *ippon*.

Left: before you start *hane goshi,* you need to get a good, tough grip with both hands. Grab as much of the material of your opponent's *gi* as you can. Here Yone is throwing to his left. For a left-side *hane goshi,* your left hand grabs your opponent's collar; your right hand grabs his lapel. Experienced judo players fight for their grips. So should you.

Center: his spring complete, Yone starts pulling his opponent onto his hips with his arms. Notice how Yone bends that left leg slightly. With that bent leg, he is going to knock his opponent's left leg out from under him.

HANE GOSHI

Hane goshi requires quickness. In order to throw a player with this technique, you must have better than average speed. As in all hip throws, you step in with one foot, pivot on that foot and bring the other foot deep inside your opponent's legs. In *hane goshi,* you whirl and spring inside your opponent's legs. Then your bent leg brushes your opponent's leg out from under him as you pull him onto

Opposite right: Yone slams into his opponent, pulling furiously with his arms to get his opponent onto his hips.

Above: merely by following through with his powerful spring, Yone lifts his opponent up high, ready to drop him to the mat.

your hip. From that point on, you simply roll him off with your arms.

Springing quickly and accurately inside your opponent's legs takes practice. You can spring into the step and pivot to get a faster entry with *harai goshi, ippon seoi nage, seoi nage* and *koshi garuma*. The very fact that you are leaping explosively into your throw will make your attack not only faster but also sharper and more focused.

TSURI KOMI GOSHI

If you see that your opponent is too erect or off his feet by a fraction, that's the time to attack with *tsuri komi goshi*. With this throw, you are trying to push him further off his feet, unweighting him. Then you pull him onto your hips and throw him.

Left: Yone steps inside with his right foot, pivoting on that foot, and simultaneously grabs a lot of his opponent's collar with his right hand. He takes a firm grip on the collar because he'll be lifting his opponent up with that hand.

Center: as Yone comes in, his hips are low. And as he pulls his opponent onto his hips, he'll straighten his legs to give himself extra lifting power. Notice how powerfully his left hand and arm are pulling his opponent's right arm out and up. Yone's right hand virtually straight-arms his opponent's neck, pushing him upward. This is the most distinctive aspect of the throw.

Tsuri komi goshi and *sode tsuri komi goshi* are both remarkably good counterthrows. For instance, when someone has tried an *osoto gari* and missed, he is especially vulnerable to *sode tsuri komi goshi*.

A word about the difference in these two throws. *Sode* means sleeve, so in *sode tsuri komi goshi*, you lift your opponent with his sleeve. In *tsuri komi goshi*, you lift him by his collar.

Opposite, right: with his right hand pushing his opponent up, Yone has put his hips solidly into his opponent's legs. He is ready to throw.

Below: to throw him over his hips, Yone now pulls with both arms. The result is a clean fall.

SODE TSURI KOMI GOSHI

Your opponent may quickly move in on you, attempting to choke you out while you are both standing up. This is easy to counter, as you will see in the following photographs.

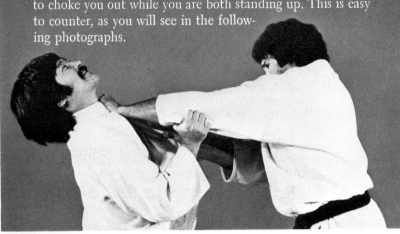

At left: first you must twist away from your opponent's choke. At the same time, bring your arm under his choking arm and grab his elbow.

Below, left: next, bring your left foot around behind you and place it between your opponent's legs. Because *sode tsuri komi goshi* is a hip throw, the footwork will be the same as for an *ogoshi* or a *harai goshi*.

Below, center: pushing mightily on your opponent's choking arm, throw him over your back. At this point, your left hand should be pulling on your opponent's other arm.

Below, right: in one fluid movement, pull your opponent across your back.

UCHI MATA

Here Yone demonstrates why he is an exquisite master of *uchi mata*. In a whirling blur of white that only a high-speed sequence camera can capture, Yone is caught at that precise instance of entry into *uchi mata*. He has pivoted with one foot and is springing deeply in between his opponent's legs with the other; his arms are starting the pull that will eventually pull the opponent onto his hips.

Uchi mata is a classic throw involving the utmost in speed, coordination and power, all released at the same moment. To sense the opportunity for such a throw and to execute it well requires concentration and
clarity of thought.
A cool, clear head
is essential.

"*Uchi mata* is
my favorite attack
against an extreme
jigo tai stance, one
with the legs wide
apart," says Yone. "It is
also very good against a
taller opponent. First,
get a strong grip and
pull a taller oppo-
nent down by the
neck. This is the
moment for
uchi mata."

Sensing that his opponent is vulnerable, Yone picks up his left foot to start his *uchi mata*.

You must get deep inside his legs to avoid striking him in the groin. Judo is a sport, and at no time must you risk injuring another player.

Yone is pivoting on his right foot as he brings his left foot around. Now he will thrust it deep between his opponent's legs as he hops back with his right foot. Some players step; Yone hops because he believes it adds speed to his move.

Deep inside and under his opponent, a position which is critical to the success of the throw, Yone pulls his opponent onto his hip with his arms. Now he straightens out that left foot (the one between his opponent's thighs) in order to sweep it up against his opponent.

Yone is actually bouncing his opponent onto his hip and then twisting him off and over onto the mat. As the opponent starts to fall, Yone's concentration is unbroken. He aims his forehead at the mat.

Once his opponent is airborne, Yone completes twisting him off his hip and drops him to the mat. Yone's total concentration makes his *uchi mata* a formidable weapon against any judo player.

SOTO MAKIKOMI

Many judo players use a stiff arm to keep opponents from getting in close, much as a football player uses a straight arm on a would-be tackler. *Soto makikomi* is a formidable weapon against such an opponent. The throw is also a good follow-up to an *osoto gari* or a *harai goshi* which you have tried but which your opponent has effectively blocked. In this instance, you don't return to your original position but switch in mid-action to *soto makikomi*. In effect, you wind yourself up in your opponent's body and simultaneously throw yourself at the mat. You should hit the mat on your shoulder. If you don't do the throw correctly, you'll hit the mat with your head. When *soto makikomi* is done expertly, it is a very powerful throw.

Top left: as Yone makes his initial move in, his opponent may expect a *harai goshi*. Accordingly, the opponent may brace himself, with his arm stiff and his hips thrust toward the front, to block that throw.

Top center: Yone pulls with great force against the opponent's right arm. With the other arm, he is planning to trap his opponent's right shoulder as high as possible. He pivots in order to thrust his left hip into the right hip of the opponent.

Top right: Yone stretches out his right arm, enabling him to get a high position on his opponent's shoulder. At this point his entire body is thrust back tightly against his opponent's.

Middle: once Yone gets his shoulder and hip position, he throws himself into a roll toward the mat. He is aiming his right shoulder at the mat. His opponent is being thrown, and because of the snapping motion, he will hit the mat hard.

Bottom: but notice that Yone's opponent breaks the major force of the fall by a perfectly timed mat slap.

Left: Yone has stepped slightly forward with his right foot, pivoting on that foot and bringing his left foot around and behind him. His left foot must be just outside and in front of his opponent's left foot, so that he will be able to get good leverage for the throw.

Opposite, left: with his right foot, Yone steps across his opponent's right foot. As he steps, his right arm pushes against his opponent's neck, driving him to the right. Simultaneously, Yone's left arm is pulling his opponent forward, over Yone's outstretched right leg. Notice how his right knee is bent; it is the trigger for the throw.

Center: Yone has snapped that key right leg as straight as a ramrod. His opponent's body is now forced to tumble over Yone's leg.

Right: the combination of Yone's timing, speed and such precise use of force overpowers his opponent instantaneously.

TAI OTOSHI

Tai otoshi is the throw so dramatically illustrated on the cover of this book. This throw demonstrates the entire spirit of judo, its gentle use of force, its meticulous sense of timing and the clever use of another person's strength. *Tai otoshi* is a gentle technique because it involves timing and coordination, not enormous strength.

First of all, it can be executed quickly, with little more than a pivot. No steps are needed. It is therefore a fast, effective move against someone who, just for a split second, might be caught leaning forward. It is also a good move against a taller, heavier opponent because against a smaller player, the taller, heavier player has to bend over or lean forward, leaving himself open for *tai otoshi*.

In this throw you either make your opponent put his weight on one foot, then step across his legs with the other one, or push his torso onto that one foot and pull him forward across your outstretched leg. In other words, you trip him.

73

TOMOE NAGE

Tomoe nage demonstrates how one gives way to his opponent's aggressive pushing. You have probably seen *tomoe nage* a hundred times—in movies, on television or even on the stage. It is a spectacular throw. Suddenly one player is thrown high over the other's head, seemingly without effort.

Tomoe nage is a sacrifice throw, because if you miss, you are vulnerable. The throw is designed to take overwhelming advantage of a person who rushes in to attack you. As he presses in at you, you step in closer to him, grab his lapels

Left: as your opponent rushes at you, step in toward him. Your left foot should be between your opponent's legs. Swing your right foot out and up in preparation for implanting it in his stomach. You should have a good, solid grip on your opponent's lapels.

Right: now you fall backward onto the mat. Pull strongly on his lapels, but do not exert pressure on his stomach yet. If you push with your foot too soon, you will block the throw, because your foot pressure will keep him up.

deeply and fall onto your back, placing one of your feet securely in the pit of his stomach. As you fall, pull hard on his lapels and simultaneously push your foot against his stomach. Snap your leg straight. As you push up with your foot and pull down on his lapels, he will go flying over your shoulder and land resoundingly on his back.

It is a perfect throw for a small person to use against a heavier, taller opponent. It is also a good throw to use when your opponent is in a deep defensive crouch, as it enables you to go in and under him.

Left: as you land on your back on the mat, your opponent should be directly over you. Now—and only now—snap your leg out powerfully and quickly. That will propel him into a complete somersault. Aim to throw him over one shoulder. Here Yone is throwing his opponent over his left shoulder, so he maintains that pulling pressure with the left hand and lets go with his right.

Right: with a successful *tomoe nage,* you'll throw your opponent some distance. Cleanly executed, it is spectacular to watch and extremely satisfying to the player. Like many throws in judo, *tomoe nage* is an excellent self-defense throw.

3
Hold-Down
Techniques:

OSAE KOMI WAZA

AT LEAST HALF OF JUDO is played on the mat, wrestling with an opponent, using hold-downs, armlocks and chokes. Mentally, mat work is as stimulating as the throwing techniques. The purpose of the mat techniques is simple: to control your opponent's body for a certain length of time or make him give up by tapping the mat or saying "*Mattai*," meaning "Enough." You can win by using hold-downs or making your opponent tap out with a choke or armlock.

In a hold-down you win by holding your opponent down for 25 or 30 seconds (depending on your point score in the match). Once you get a legitimate hold-down, the referee says, "*Osae komi*," indicating that the timekeeper has started counting the seconds. If your opponent then breaks the hold-down, the referee says, "*Osae komi toketa*," meaning that the holding has been stopped.

To appreciate the beauty of judo, you must think of the sport as a continuous flow of action in which you seek, by throw, choke, armlock or mat hold-down, to control your opponent.

The flow theory will especially help you to understand *osae komi waza*, the hold-downs. You can actually start thinking of a hold-down during the throw itself. If your opponent has thrown you poorly, it may be possible for you to turn and get a good hold-down on him the instant you hit the mat. And, of course, when you throw an opponent, he'll wind up on his back, a perfect opportunity for any number of mat attacks.

In attacking someone or defending yourself, you should obviously keep your body low and your weight evenly distributed. Flexibility counts. If you are too rigid, you won't be able to move quickly. Many times, in hold-downs, if you think of yourself as a deadweight, you feel a lot heavier to your opponent.

Again, think in terms of mechanics. Use leverage to try to break your opponent's leverage. If he is trying to arch his back, get control of his head. Get under his neck and try to lift it off the mat. He won't have the leverage then. Or go after his arms or legs. Prevent him from getting the leverage he needs by controlling the part of his body he is using to gain leverage.

Flexibility is also essential in mastering *osae komi waza*. You must be able to shift your weight from one part of your opponent's body to another as he changes his defense. Your aim is to remain in control by constantly shifting, using your strength to its maximum and trying to prevent your opponent from using his maximum strength.

KESA GATAME

Kesa gatame illustrates what we mean by flow. Imagine that you have just thrown an opponent with an *osoto gari*. As he falls to his back, you must "flow" into a hold-down such as *kesa gatame*. By applying it instantly when you're

77

Yone threw his opponent with an *osoto gari* a second or two before this photograph was taken. He then took advantage of the fact that his opponent was more or less on his back by simply moving quickly in to his opponent's right side to apply *kesa gatame.*

* Yone sits close to the right side of his opponent. He gains tremendous stability by spreading his legs out, keeping them slightly bent for even greater strength.

* With his right hand, he has reached around his opponent's collar as far as possible. He hasn't grabbed the collar, but keeps his hand flat on tne mat and applies pressure against the back of his opponent's head with his forearm.

* Yone's left arm traps his opponent's right arm. To make his trap effective, he grabs a lot of material from the upper sleeve of his opponent's *gi*. Note especially: he not only grips strongly but pulls the arm up, stretching it out and reducing its effectiveness.

* Bend your head down as low as you need to. Your opponent may push at your head or chin with his free left forearm. Keeping your head low will help deflect the force of such pushes.

* Try to think heavy. This isn't as ridiculous as it sounds. Concentrate on keeping your whole body low; it makes it a lot tougher for your opponent.

both on the mat, you are seizing the opportunity to maintain control of your opponent's movements.

Kesa gatame is the most common of all judo holds. Although mastering it takes time and practice, it is easy to learn and remarkably easy to use. Once mastered, *kesa gatame* becomes a formidable weapon.

You must expect several reactions from your opponent. He may try to push your head up and away with his free left arm. If he does, bend your head down and to the outside.

He may try to hook your left leg with his right leg. If he does, your hold will be considered broken. To stop him, just keep moving with him in a clockwise pattern.

If you think he is simply going to break your grip, you can lock your hands together. But you do this at your own risk because it is a good setup for your opponent to escape. The person escaping will swing both his legs from side to side, creating enough momentum to unseat you. At the same time he'll grab your belt in back and pull you onto his hip. Now—if your hands are locked together—your opponent will push his head against the mat, trapping your hands there. When he rocks, you will not be able to brace against that motion, and he will escape.

KAMI SHIHO GATAME

When a *sensei* first shows you how to execute a *kami shiho gatame*, you will wonder how you could use such a hold on anyone. Yes, it looks tough, but you will find many opportunities to use it.

For instance, if someone had gotten a *waza ari* on you with a partially successful *tomoe nage*, you could, if you turned around quickly enough, work into *kami shiho gatame*. Of course, you always work into a hold; no one is going to lie there waiting for you to get in. Work first with one hand, then the other. Fake your opponent by attempting a choke; then move in quickly.

Okay, suppose you have been thrown by a *seoi nage* and are now scrambling fast to lie on top of your opponent. First, work one of your arms under his arm, trapping it against his side. Hook the thumb of that arm into your opponent's belt. Now work the other arm under his remaining arm, also hooking your thumb into his belt.

When you have trapped his arms, think of yourself as a heavy weight pressing into your opponent. Your chin presses into his stomach, your chest against his shoulders. You can straddle his head between your legs. Or, for greater stability, stretch your legs out wide on the floor.

The top photograph, opposite, shows the hold-down with Yone straddling his opponent's head.

In the bottom photograph Yone stretches out his legs for greater stability against the twisting and turning of the man underneath. Either way you choose, you trap your opponent's arms against his sides, hooking your thumbs into his belt, and then press down with your body.

KATA GATAME

I call this the strongest hold in judo. Not only is a player held completely immobile, but he can also be choked into tapping out with *kata gatame*.

It is hard to get, of course, but the opportunity will present itself when you are holding a judo player with *kesa gatame* and he tries to elbow you or push your head away from him. As he brings that arm up across his body, release your *kesa gatame*, reach behind his outstretched arm with one hand and lock hands. Squeeze his arm into his neck. He will inevitably tap out. Simple and very effective.

As you squeeze and pull your arm together, put your head to the floor. This helps increase the pressure on your opponent.

As you get in for *kata gatame*, twist your knee in against your opponent's side to prevent him from getting away.

YOKO SHIHO GATAME

This is quite a simple hold. Anyone who has ever wrestled will recognize it as a good position for pinning. In judo, of course, you don't have to pin someone; you need only control him by keeping him on his back.

With *yoko shiho gatame*, you move in from the side at a right angle. Next, press your chest against his stomach, thinking of yourself as a heavy weight. With your right hand, reach between his legs and try to grab his belt from underneath. With your left hand, reach in and grab his collar, holding it firmly. Bring your right knee in against his waist. This will prevent him from twisting in toward you in an effort to escape. As he twists away from you, you can use your head to prevent yourself from being rolled. Or you can momentarily release your left hand from his collar to brace yourself against a roll.

4
Choking
Techniques:

SHIME WAZA

AT FIRST, the thought of choking or being choked makes beginning judo players apprehensive. It is a natural, useful element of judo, employed in conjunction with throws and hold-downs. A judo choke is pressure against the carotid artery, the jugular vein or the windpipe—or all three. And, usually, the chokes involve the use of the collar and the lapel of the *gi*.

To win by choking, you must make your opponent tap out with his hands or feet, or say "*Mattai*." You must be alert to his condition when you are choking him, for he can actually lose consciousness or lack the freedom of movement to tap.

To get a choke, you must move fast, getting your grip without being too obvious, and choke quickly and strongly. You should have complete control over your opponent so he is unable to break away.

As you gain experience, you will instinctively look for opportunities in which to use the choke or in which you can distract your opponent by faking a choke and then going on to another strategy.

A word of warning: At any sign of surrender, release your

84

opponent at once. The *sensei* will start artificial respiration if by any chance your opponent becomes unconscious.

Escaping a Choke

The best way to escape a choke is to keep your chin down, guarding your neck from a stranglehold; don't let yourself fall into a vulnerable position. In certain instances you can use your arms to push or twist away the elbow of your opponent's choking arm. In other situations, you may have to tap out.

GIYAKU JUJI JIME

It can be an advantage to be on the bottom in judo, particularly when you can apply *giyaku juji jime*. It is a fundamental choke, one that is used quite often; it consists of reaching deep inside your opponent's collar with crossed hands, then applying pressure against the sides of his neck.

Left: work your right hand in deep on your opponent's right collar, in grabbing position, with your fingers inside and your thumb on the outside. Your left hand should be in equally deep on your opponent's left collar.

Right: to choke your opponent, simply bring your hands together and bring him down on your chest. If you are on top of your opponent, lean over his head; it makes the choke more effective.

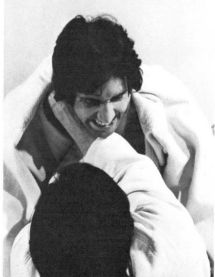

KATA JUJI JIME

The *kata* choke is a minor variation on *giyaku,* the basic cross choke. It, too, can be used either when your opponent is on top or when you are on top.

Let's assume that you are underneath your opponent. Quickly, move to grab his left collar with your left hand, placing your thumb on the outside of the lapel. Get deep enough; otherwise you won't have enough leverage to do the choking. With your right hand, cross over and grab his right lapel deep, this time with your thumb on the inside and the fingers outside.

The choking action takes place when you twist your left hand so that the thumb on the outside of the lapel now touches your opponent's neck. Pull him toward you with your right hand. If the squeezing action is at all effective, your opponent will become uncomfortable immediately. Once a choke is applied effectively, he'll become red in the face and will undoubtedly tap out.

Left: see how the positions of the hands are reversed—left thumb out, right thumb in.

Bottom left: Yone goes deep before twisting his opponent's left collar for the choke.

Bottom right: Yone pulls his opponent down onto his chest; he uses his legs to prevent his opponent from rolling or twisting away from the choke.

HADAKA JIME

Once you get this choke on an opponent, he is not going to break it easily. If he is careless enough to let you move in on him from the rear, quickly place your right hand across his throat. Quickly, before he realizes what's going on.

You have to get your right hand across before he starts to defend his throat by bringing his chin down. Then reach over his left shoulder with your left hand. Lock both palms together and pull back against your opponent's throat.

This is a variation of *hadaka jime.* You simply use your arms a bit differently to achieve the choke. Your right arm still slides in front of your opponent's throat, but the difference is that your left arm is positioned on your opponent's left shoulder, locking your right hand in your left elbow. Your left hand pushes against your opponent's head. This lock creates powerful leverage, making this variation even more devastating than the basic *hadaka jime.*

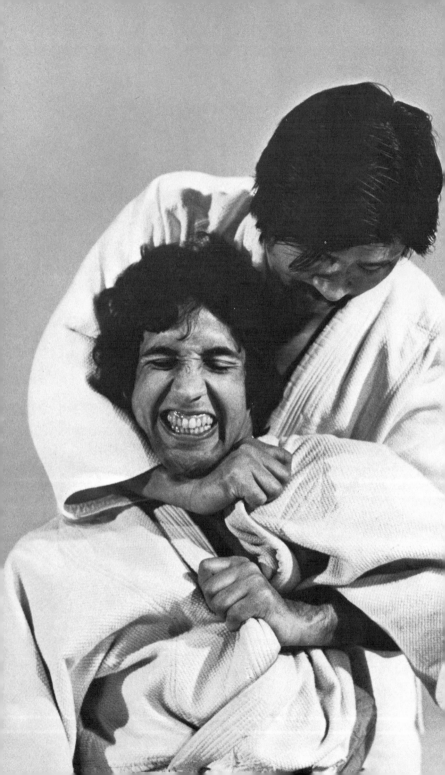

OKERI ERI JIME

Okeri eri jime is simple, very strong and relatively easy to get in a variety of positions.

One hand slides across your opponent's throat and locks onto the lapel of the *gi;* your thumb will be inside. Your other hand goes underneath his other arm and pulls down on his opposite collar. So one hand chokes by putting the thin edge of your wrist against his throat; the other hand traps him in that position by maintaining pressure on the other lapel of the *gi.*

If you are lying down, wrap your legs around his waist and stretch backward. This will stretch his body out, making it just about impossible for him to escape.

The best opportunity for *okeri eri jime* comes when you and your opponent are kneeling side by side on the mat. It happens very often. Put your hands in the choking position and sit down, much the way a wrestler sits out. It's extremely effective and catches many opponents unawares.

Notice that the thumb of the choking hand is on the inside. The other hand goes under the opponent's arm and grabs the opposite lapel.

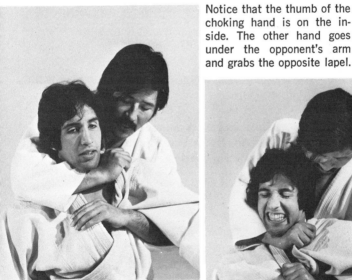

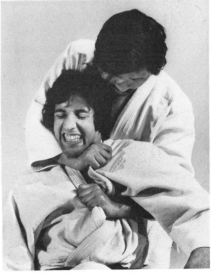

The pressure's on.

5
Armlock
Techniques:

KANSETSU WAZA

IN COMPETITION, armlock techniques are used only by brown- or black-belt players; however, in *randori* some instructors encourage their practice. Armlocks are excellent moves for self-defense. Again, they involve the principle of the lever. And again, armlocks are used with other techniques of judo. For instance, there is one armlock to be used after a throw and there is another to be used when a player lunges at you.

Kansetsu waza are techniques of applying pressure to the elbow; to prevent injuries, such pressure should be applied gradually. The main point is to gain complete control over your opponent's arm and force submission.

But there is some danger here: if you are attacked with an armlock, you should either escape or submit quickly to avoid any chance of injury.

WAKI GATAME

You must always look for an opportunity to use *waki gatame*. This armlock is the classic defense against a knife-wielding attacker. If your judo opponent approaches you with one arm outstretched, he could be vulnerable to an armlock such as *waki gatame*. It is a surprise move; few people expect it.

Pull your opponent's arm sharply toward you, stepping around to the side. Put one arm under the elbow of your opponent; put the other hand on the wrist of the exposed arm. Next, lock your free hand into his wrist. You now have the leverage to bend your opponent's arm against his elbow, a painful maneuver which automatically ends the point. Few judo players will risk injury and try to hold out, for it would be foolish. Yone is exerting pressure here, and his opponent is already tapping out.

UDE GATAME

A straight armlock such as *ude gatame* can be applied in a variety of positions. It requires lightning speed. Simply grab your opponent's wrist, pull it out straight, twist it and apply the pressure against his elbow. Be careful when you practice this; a mistake is painful.

The key is to keep your opponent's arm outstretched. Then grab his elbow with both hands, exerting pressure in toward your own body. You can prevent your opponent from rolling out by keeping one knee on his body.

JUJI GATAME

This is a superb illustration of seizing an opportunity in judo. Here, you can see the flow of judo, from the throw to the offensive attack on the mat. By following your opponent down quickly you can then go into an armlock, choke or hold-down.

Left: the player has held onto the right wrist of the man he has just thrown. He then pulls up hard on his opponent's arm.

Center: he sits down suddenly, as close as he can to his opponent's shoulder. With his left foot, he steps over his opponent's head.

Right: now, he leans back on the mat, squeezing his opponent's elbow between his knees. In order to apply pressure, he arches back and twists the opponent's arm in the direction of the little finger of that hand.

93

Glossary

ATEMI WAZA—Techniques for striking vital points of an opponent's body; an illegal art

DO-JIME—Body scissors to apply pressure; an illegal art

DOJO—A place to practice judo

FUSENSHO—Win by default

GATAME—Holding technique used in mat work

GI—Coat and pants worn by judo players

HAJIME—Begin

HANTEI—Referee's call for a decision

HIKI WAKE—Draw

IPPON—A full point

JIGO TAI—Defensive stance

JUDOKA—One who practices judo

JUJITSU—Ancient system of self-defense

KAKE—Application of a technique

KANSETSU WAZA—Armlock techniques

KATA—Formal technique

KATAME WAZA—Grappling techniques

94

KUZUSHI—The point at which opponent's balance is completely broken

MATTAI—Signal of submission, enough

MATE—Wait, stop

NAGE WAZA—Throwing techniques

OSAE KOMI—Start of hold-down; timekeeper's signal

OSAE KOMI TOKETA—Hold is broken

OSAE KOMI WAZA—Holding techniques

RANDORI—Free play; fighting practice

REI—A bow

SAMURAI—Feudal warrior of Japan

SENSEI—Instructor

SHIAI—Contest

SHIME WAZA—Choking techniques

SHIZEN TAI—Offensive stance

SONOMAMA—Freeze in the position you are in at time of call

TACHI REI—Standing bow

UCHIKOMI—Form practice

UKEMI—Falling technique

WAZA—Techniques

WAZA ARI—Half-point

YUSEGACHI—Win by superiority

ZA-REI—Bow from the sitting position

Judo Ranks

BEGINNER	JUNIOR (*Under 17*)	SENIOR
6th Kyu (Novice)	White Belt (Novice)	White Belt (Novice)
5th Kyu	Yellow Belt	Yellow Belt
4th Kyu	Orange Belt	Green Belt
3rd Kyu	Green Belt	Brown Belt
2nd Kyu	Blue Belt	Brown Belt
1st Kyu (Advanced)	Purple Belt (Advanced)	Brown Belt (Advanced)

BLACK-BELT RANKS

1st	Shodan	6th	Rokudan
2nd	Hidan	7th	Shichidan
3rd	Sandan	8th	Hachidan
4th	Yodan	9th	Kudan
5th	Godan	10th	Judan (Advanced)